The Story of Cars

Words by Howard W. Kanetzke

Juvenile Publications Editor
State Historical Society of Wisconsin

Raintree Childrens Books
Milwaukee • Toronto • Melbourne • London

Library of Congress Number: 77-27533

    3 4 5 6 7 8 9 0 82 81 80

Printed and bound in the United States of America.

Library of Congress Cataloging in Publication Data

Kanetzke, Howard W.
    The story of cars.

    (Read about)
    Bibliography: p.
    Includes index.
    SUMMARY: An introduction to the history of
automobiles with a description of how they work,
how they are produced, and some of the different
kinds and their uses.
    1. Automobiles — Juvenile literature.
[1. Automobiles] I. Title.
TL147.M6   629.22'22   77-27533
ISBN 0-8393-0086-7 lib. bdg.

The Story
of Cars

For hundreds of years people traveled in carriages. Most carriages were pulled by horses. Roman chariots were small and fast. One or two horses pulled them easily.

chariot

Horse-drawn carriages were used by many people until the 1900s. Large, heavy carriages used many horses.

carriage

steam carriage

This carriage was powered by a steam engine. Early trains also had steam engines. This steam carriage was heavy. It moved slowly. Horse-drawn carriages were just as fast as steam carriages.

Benz

The first cars to work well were powered by gasoline engines. Cars still use gasoline today.

The Benz was an early car with a modern engine. It had three wheels. Soon, many other kinds of cars were built. Some had four wheels. A few had hoods. Most early cars did not have a roof.

People began to build stronger bodies
for the cars. Early cars had wooden frames.
The frames were covered with metal plates.
Then padded seats were put in. Sometimes
a hood was put on the back of the car.

Early cars were noisy. They moved
faster than horse-drawn carriages. Cars
frightened people who were used to horses.
Some people came to stare at cars as they
went by. Others ran inside and hid.

Early cars were dangerous in towns.
They were fast and noisy. People had to run
out of their way. Cars were hard to steer.
Sometimes the brakes did not work well.
Then cars skidded.

At first, only a few people had money to buy cars. Each car took a long time to make. This made cars expensive.

Henry Ford found a way to change this. He made many cars quickly on an assembly line. He made the first low-cost car. It was called the Model T.

On the assembly line, each worker put one part of the car in place. The next person in line added another part. The workers had to do their jobs quickly.

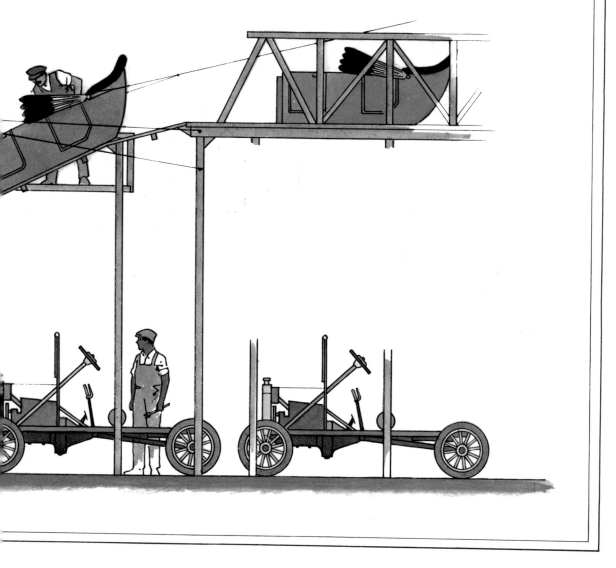

The first cars were not comfortable. The car body rested on metal leaf springs. This is called the suspension. The old leaf springs were stiff. Some early tires were made of solid rubber. They were hard.

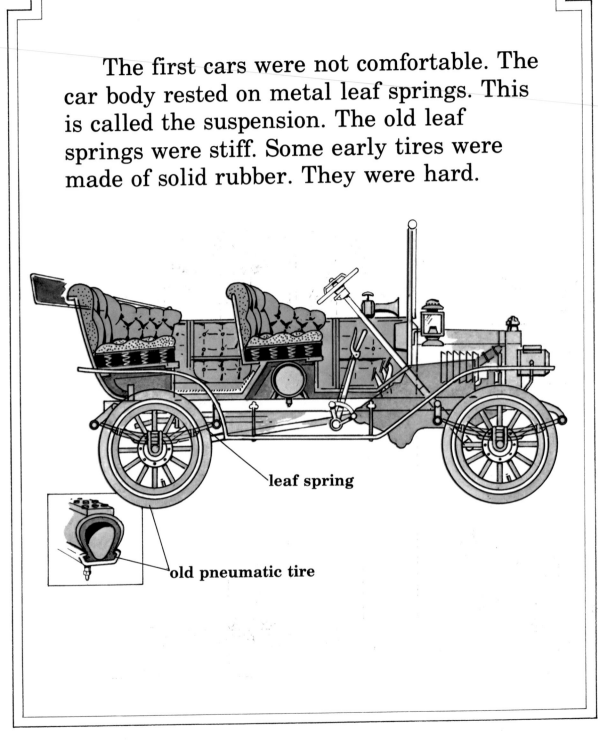

leaf spring

old pneumatic tire

Cars today are much more comfortable. Their suspensions have coiled springs. The seats are soft. Tires today are pneumatic tires. This means they have air inside.

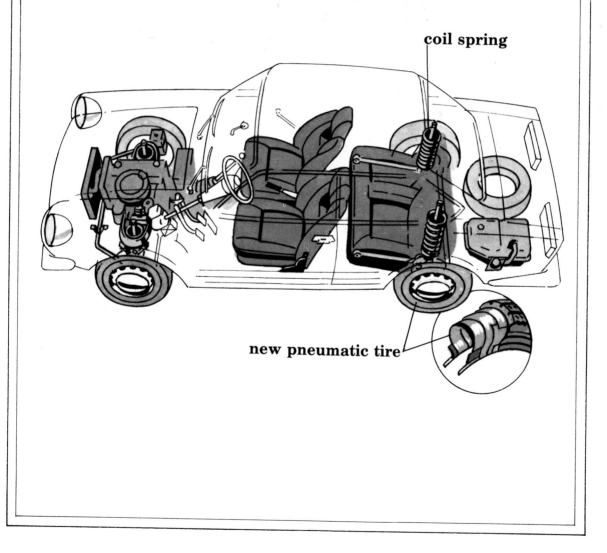

coil spring

new pneumatic tire

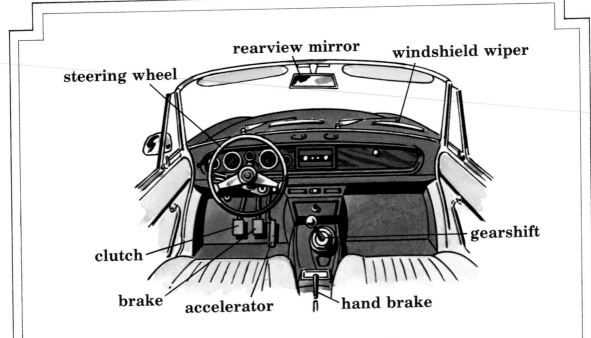

rearview mirror

windshield wiper

steering wheel

gearshift

clutch

brake   accelerator   hand brake

Every car has controls for the driver to use. To turn the car, the driver turns the steering wheel. It is linked to the wheels. The driver presses the gas pedal (accelerator) to make the car go faster. Pushing the brake pedal makes the car stop. The brakes are linked to the wheels.

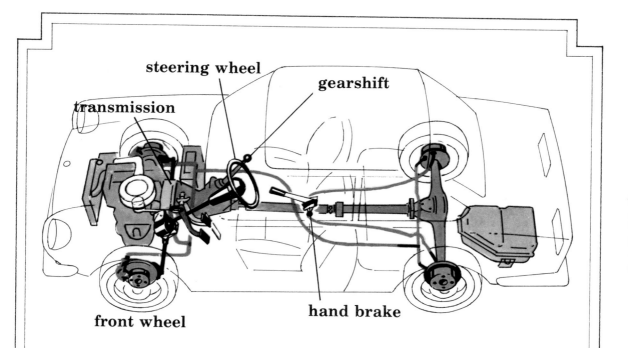

steering wheel

gearshift

transmission

hand brake

front wheel

The transmission is what makes the car move forward or backward. Cars can have either automatic or manual transmissions. With an automatic transmission, the driver puts the gearshift lever on "drive" or "reverse." Then the driver presses the gas pedal. Some cars have a manual transmission. Then the driver must use the clutch and gearshift to make the car move.

The driver starts the engine. Gasoline
begins to flow through a pipe from the
gasoline tank to the carburetor. The
carburetor turns the gasoline into a vapor.
The vapor is sent to the cylinders. In each
cylinder there is a spark plug. Sparks from
the plug make the vapor explode. This
happens in one cylinder at a time. Inside
the cylinders are pistons. The exploding
vapor forces the pistons down.

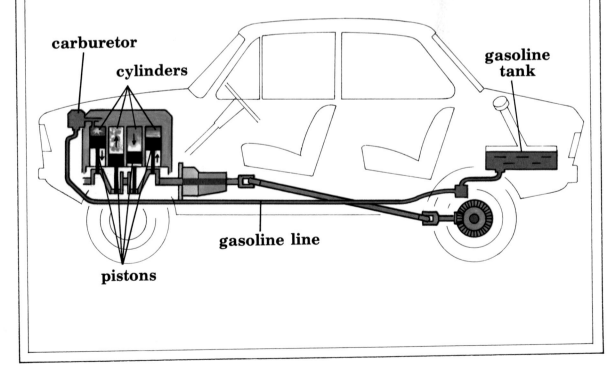

carburetor

cylinders

gasoline
tank

gasoline line

pistons

As pistons move, they turn the crankshaft. The crankshaft is connected to the driveshaft. The driveshaft turns the rear axle. The rear axle turns the rear wheels. The rear wheels move the car.

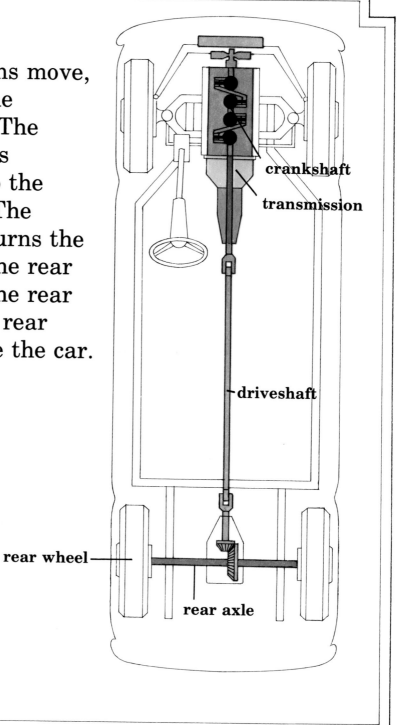

crankshaft

transmission

driveshaft

rear wheel

rear axle

some stages on an assembly line

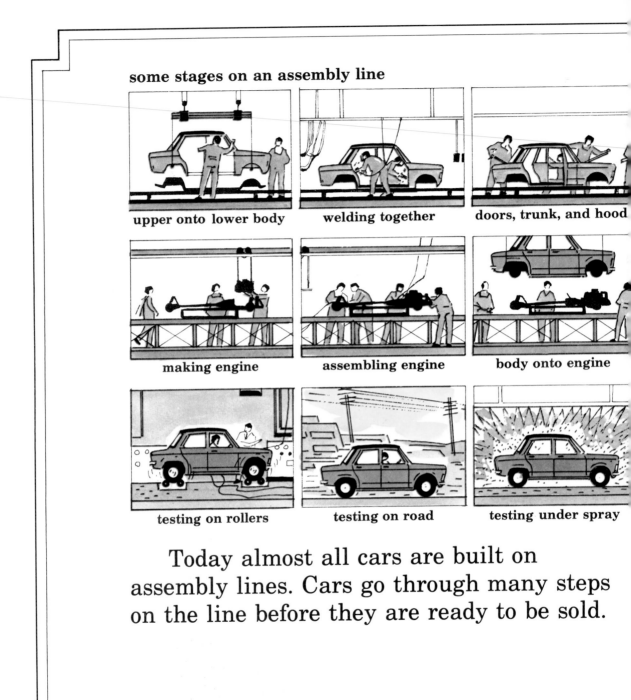

upper onto lower body

welding together

doors, trunk, and hood

making engine

assembling engine

body onto engine

testing on rollers

testing on road

testing under spray

Today almost all cars are built on
assembly lines. Cars go through many steps
on the line before they are ready to be sold.

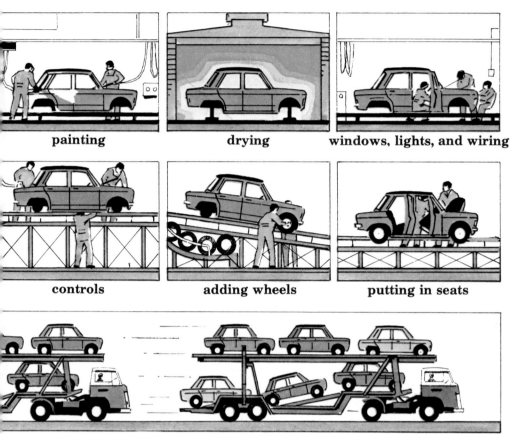

painting   drying   windows, lights, and wiring

controls   adding wheels   putting in seats

distributing

Each worker on the assembly line learns one special job. The car moves along the line from one person to the next. By the end of the line, the car is finished. Then it can be tested.

New models of cars come out every year. Each new model must be carefully planned and tested.

One or two test cars will be made in the new style. They will be tested in different kinds of weather.

mountain test

desert test

crash test

A test car is checked for strength. It may be crashed against a wall. Then the makers see how much it has been hurt. A car must pass all the tests. Then it can be made on an assembly line. New cars are often shown to the public at automobile shows.

automobile show

German Volkswagen

Cars come in many different sizes. Some cars can be big. They use a lot of gasoline. Small cars use less gasoline. More and more smaller cars are now being built.

British Mini

Italian Fiat

French "deux chevaux"

Cars have different shapes. People want many different styles of cars. Most people have sedans. People who want more space can buy station wagons. Some cars are big enough to have beds inside. They are called campers. People who want cars that are fast and powerful buy sports cars.

sedan

station wagon

camper

sports car

Car racing is a popular sport. The first races were from one town to another. Cars like this one were built just for racing.

early racing car

Some races are still held on roads.
These races are called rallies.
These cars are in the Monte Carlo rally.
The roads in this rally twist and turn and
climb up mountains.

Monte Carlo rally

Most races today are run on special tracks. Racing cars are built only for racing. They do not look like ordinary cars. They can go at very high speeds on the racetrack.

This car was built for speed. It is called The Blue Flame. It is a supersonic car. That means it can go faster than the speed of sound. The Blue Flame can travel as fast as some jet airplanes.

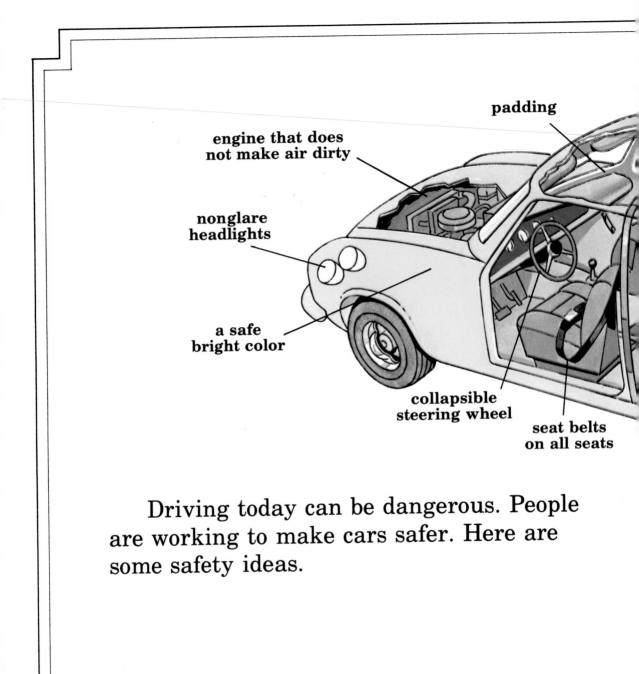

padding

**engine that does
not make air dirty**

**nonglare
headlights**

**a safe
bright color**

**collapsible
steering wheel**

**seat belts
on all seats**

Driving today can be dangerous. People are working to make cars safer. Here are some safety ideas.

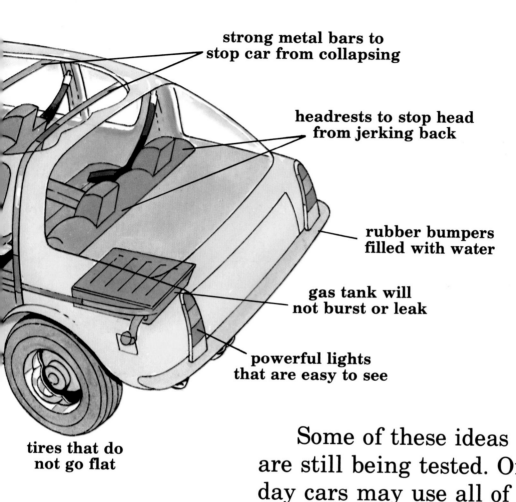

strong metal bars to
stop car from collapsing

headrests to stop head
from jerking back

rubber bumpers
filled with water

gas tank will
not burst or leak

powerful lights
that are easy to see

tires that do
not go flat

Some of these ideas
are still being tested. One
day cars may use all of
them. They will help to
protect people when
accidents happen.

There are millions of cars on the roads today. Roads are sometimes blocked by traffic jams like this.

Cars in cities can be dangerous. When cars are running, they give off some poisonous gas. Many cars together could poison the air. Inspectors in some cities wear masks. These inspectors are finding out how much poison is in the gas from one car. Controls are now used in cars to check poisonous gas.

electric cars

jet car

People are trying to build new kinds of cars. These are electric cars. They run on batteries instead of gasoline. They do not poison the air. Electric cars today are too slow to be used by many people. If they can be made to run faster, they may someday be used by everyone.

Someday cars might even have jet engines like those in jet airplanes. People have planned how to make jet cars like this one. New kinds of cars must be tested for a long time before they can be used.

The Metric System

In the United States, things are measured in inches, pounds, quarts, and so on. Most countries of the world use centimeters, kilograms, and liters for these things. The United States uses the American system to measure things. Most other countries use the metric system. By 1985, the United States will be using the metric system, too.

In some books, you will see two systems of measurement. For example, you might see a sentence like this: "That bicycle wheel is 27 inches (69 centimeters) across." When all countries have changed to the metric system, inches will not be used any more. But until then, you may sometimes have to change measurements from one system to the other. The chart on the next page will help you.

All you have to do is multiply the unit of measurement in Column 1 by the number in Column 2. That gives you the unit in Column 3.

Suppose you want to change 5 inches to centimeters. First, find inches in Column 1. Next, multiply 5 times 2.54. You get 12.7. So, 5 inches is 12.7 centimeters.

Column 1	Column 2	Column 3
THIS UNIT OF MEASUREMENT	TIMES THIS NUMBER	GIVES THIS UNIT OF MEASUREMENT
inches	2.54	centimeters
feet	30.	centimeters
feet	.3	meters
yards	.9	meters
miles	1.6	kilometers
ounces	28.	grams
pounds	.45	kilograms
fluid ounces	.03	liters
pints	.47	liters
quarts	.95	liters
gallons	3.8	liters
centimeters	.4	inches
meters	1.1	yards
kilometers	.6	miles
grams	.035	ounces
kilograms	2.2	pounds
liters	33.8	fluid ounces
liters	2.1	pints
liters	1.06	quarts
liters	.26	gallons

Where to Read About
the Story of Cars

Pronunciation Key

a	a as in **cat, bad**
ā	a as in **able**, ai as in **train**, ay as in **play**
ä	a as in **father, car**, o as in **cot**
e	e as in **bend, yet**
ē	e as in **me**, ee as in **feel**, ea as in **beat**, ie as in **piece**, y as in **heavy**
i	i as in **in, pig**, e as in **pocket**
ī	i as in **ice, time**, ie as in **tie**, y as in **my**
o	o as in **top**, a as in **watch**
ō	o as in **old**, oa as in **goat**, ow as in **slow**, oe as in **toe**
ô	o as in **cloth**, au as in **caught**, aw as in **paw**, a as in **all**
oo	oo as in **good**, u as in **put**
o͞o	oo as in **tool**, ue as in **blue**
oi	oi as in **oil**, oy as in **toy**
ou	ou as in **out**, ow as in **plow**
u	u as in **up, gun**, o as in **other**
ur	ur as in **fur**, er as in **person**, ir as in **bird**, or as in **work**
yo͞o	u as in **use**, ew as in **few**
ə	a as in **again**, e as in **broken**, i as in **pencil**, o as in **attention**, u as in **surprise**
ch	ch as in **such**
ng	ng as in **sing**
sh	sh as in **shell, wish**
th	th as in **three, bath**
t͟h	th as in **that, together**

GLOSSARY

These words are defined the way they are used in this book

accelerator (ak sel′ ə rā′tər) a pedal
on a car which is pressed to make the
car go faster

accident (ak′ sə dənt) something that is
not expected; when a car breaks down or
is damaged

assembly line (ə sem′ blē līn′) a system
for making cars where each worker has
a special part of the car to make

automatic (ô tə mat′ ik) working by
itself; without outside control

automobile (ô′ tə mə bēl′) a car; a
vehicle with four wheels, usually
powered by a gasoline engine

axle (ak′ səl) a bar on which a pair of
wheels turn

battery (bat′ ər ē) a device containing
chemicals which make an electric current

body (bod′ ē) the main or central part
of something

brake (brāk) something used to slow or stop
the movement of a vehicle; to make
something slow down or stop by using
a brake

camper (kam′ pər) a large car often
used for camping

carburetor (kär′ bə rā tər) the part of an
engine in which gasoline and air are mixed

carriage (kar′ ij) a vehicle without a
motor that moves on wheels

chariot (char′ ē ət) a two-wheeled
carriage drawn by horses

clutch (kluch) a device in a car which
allows the gears to shift

coil (koil) to wind around and around

comfortable (kum′ fər tə bəl) giving
comfort

connect (kə nekt′) to join things together

control (kən trōl′) to be able to direct
or have power over a thing

crankshaft (krangk′ shaft′) a bar that
connects with other bars to turn
the wheels of a car

crash (krash) to collide violently with something

cylinder (sil′ ən dər) a long, rounded, hollow object

drive shaft (drīv′ shaft′) a bar that turns the rear axle of a car

electric (i lek′ trik) being run by electricity

engine (en′ jin) a machine that makes use of energy to run other machines

expensive (eks pen′ siv) costing a lot of money

explode (eks plōd′) to burst out suddenly; to burn very quickly

flow (flō) to move in a stream

gas (gas) a substance like air that is neither solid nor liquid

gasoline (gas′ ə lēn′) a liquid fuel used in the engines of cars, trucks, and airplanes

gas tank (gas tangk) a container in a car which holds gasoline

gear (gēr) part of a car's transmission

which allows the car to move forward
at a certain speed

gearshift (gēr′ shift′) the part of a car
that joins the gears and the motor

hood (hood) the metal cover over the
engine of a car

horse-drawn (hôrs′ drôn′) pulled by
one or more horses

inexpensive (in′ eks pen′ siv) not costing
much money; not expensive

jet airplane (jet′   er′ plān) an airplane
driven by a jet engine

link (lingk) to join or connect at
some point

manual (man′ yoo əl) being done by
hand; not automatic

mask (mask) a covering worn over the
face to protect or hide it

metal (met′ əl) a substance that is usually
hard and has a shiny surface, and is used
to make many objects and machines

modern (mod′ ərn) belonging to the
present time

piston (pis′ tən) part of a car engine which moves back and forth

plate (plāt) a flat piece of a hard material, such as metal

pneumatic (nōō mat′ ik) being filled with air

poison (poi′ zən) a substance that causes sickness or death when taken into the body; to fill something with poison

poisonous (poi′ zə nəs) causing sickness or death by poison

popular (pop′ yə lər) liked by many people

powerful (pou′ ər fəl) having great power

press (pres) to push steadily on something

racetrack (rās′ trak′) a track used for racing

rally (ral′ ē) a car race run on ordinary roads

rear (rēr) the back part of a thing

safety (sāf′ tē) giving freedom from danger

sedan (si dan′) a medium-sized car with a roof and seats in the front and back

skid (skid) to slide sideways

spark (spärk) a short, bright flash of
electricity

speed (spēd) a rate of motion; quick
or fast motion

sports car (spôrts kär) a fast, powerful
kind of car

spring (spring) a device, often made
of coiled wire, that will move back
to its original shape after being bent

stage (stāj) one step in a process that
is made of many steps

stare (ster) to look for a long time
at something

steam engine (stēm′ en′ jin) an engine
run by steam

steer (stēr) to guide the direction in
which something is moving

stiff (stif) not moving or bending easily

strength (strength) the quality of
being strong

style (stīl) a particular kind of design
or way of building something

supersonic (so͞o′ pər sän′ ik) past the
  speed of sound

suspension (sə spen′ shən) the springs in
  a car which make the ride more comfortable

system (sis′ təm) an orderly way of
  doing things

test (test) to use something in order
  to find out its quality

track (trak) a road built specially
  as a racecourse

traffic jam (traf′ ik jam′) a situation
  where many vehicles are crowded onto
  a road and are moving slowly or stopped

transmission (trans mish′ ən) a system
  of gears in an automobile which allows
  it to move

travel (trav′ əl) to make a trip from one
  place to another; to move

tricycle (trī′ si kəl) a vehicle with
  three wheels, two in the back and one
  in the front

twist (twist) to move back and forth in
  a winding motion

vapor (vā′ pər) small particles like
steam or smoke that can be seen floating
in the air

wall (wôl) a solid, upright, flat structure
used to divide or protect an area

waste (wāst) to use up in a careless way

Bibliography

Butler, Hal. *Millions of Cars*. New York: Julian Messner, 1972.

Butterworth, William E. *Dave White and the Electric Wonder Car*. New York: Four Winds Press, 1974.

Georgano, G. N. *The Complete Encyclopedia of Motor Cars*. New York: E. P. Dutton, 1973.

Harris, Leon A. *Behind the Scenes in a Car Factory*. Philadelphia: J. B. Lippincott Co., 1972.

Klein, Aaron E. *Auto Mechanics: An Introduction and Guide*. New York: Franklin Watts, 1974.

Koren, Edward. *Behind the Wheel*. New York: Holt, Rinehart and Winston, 1972.

Liebers, Arthur. *You Can Be a Professional Driver*. New York: Lothrop, Lee and Shepard, 1976.

Olyslager, Piet. *Illustrated Motor Cars of the World*. New York: Grosset and Dunlap, Inc., 1971.

Stambler, Irwin. *Automobile Engines of Today and Tomorrow*. New York: Grosset and Dunlap, Inc., 1972.